The Color of Goodbye

The Color of Goodbye

Poems by

Pattie Palmer-Baker

Cover design by Shay Culligan

ISBN: 978-1-954353-34-3

Kelsay Books
502 South 1040 East, A-119
American Fork, Utah, 84003

John Morrison, my teacher and friend
MK Moen, my supporter and friend
Caroline Martin, my editor and friend

Acknowledgments

Many thanks to the publications in which versions of the following poems have appeared, occasionally with different titles:

As You Were (Military Experience and the Arts, Fall/Winter 2016): "Don't"

Bacopa Literary Review (2017): "My Mother's Hands"

Calyx: "1943"

Dove Tales: "Oh Momma, Tell Me Where You Are"

Ghazalpage (Summer 2015): "Goodbye to Once Before"

Phantom Drift (2019): "Death Takes My Mother," "The Hereafter"

She Holds the Face of the World (10th-anniversary VoiceCatcher anthology, 2016): "The Hand-Off"

Understanding Suicide, Living with Loss. Paths to Prevention (2019): "Like Father, Like Daughter"

Contents

1943

Home on leave, my father-to-be
crisp in navy whites dances
to *Harbor Lights* with my mother
at the Biltmore Hotel.
I am the shadow behind his fingers
touching her war-trimmed waist.
I crouch in the negative space
where her head sinks into his chest.
I float in the champagne bubbles
broken on the roofs of their mouths.
I dust the navy-blue gloves sized small
crumpled on the floor.
I am the run in her ruined silk stockings.
I hollow the pillow where her head rocks.
I swim into the curl of her tidal-waved thoughts.
I am a blond mote lodged in her eye.
She can't blink me out.

Don't Go

Don't, Daddy,
don't volunteer.
You won't be able to endure.
You have an unarmored heart—
hidden so well,
even you can't find it.

Don't go.
You will be sent to New Guinea.
Your boys, with the eyes of men,
will dig dirt, saw wood, tote steel.
At night, as you choke on the thick black heat,
you will hear branches crack, leaves whiffle,
and you will wonder—
A spiny anteater?
A fruit bat?
A spider bigger than your fist?
Or a Japanese soldier,
deadly as the death adder snake?

You alone—
you will believe—carry
the deadweight of all those men.
You will turn yourself inside out.
Wounded boys, dead boys
will tear pieces off your heart
beating on your shirtless chest.

If you go,
your body will come home,
but not that honeyed promise of a man.
So little of your heart will remain,
my mother, sisters and I will starve.
You will seek someone, anything
to jump-start that weak, tattered heart.
Jim Beam will be his name,
a golden-tongued serial killer.

Don't go.
One day, years in the future,
you will sit at the head
of the kitchen table
drunk,
and you will break the cease-fire
in place for eighteen years.
You will sob,
Oh, the boys, all the boys—
dead.

Stars without the Shine

With eyes tender and fierce,
my father oversees the wells
in the Masjid-i-Suleiman* oil field.
Before the heat bleaches the cobalt sky white,
his blue eyes trace
crisscrossed towers that reach up
to graze the rim of his world.

Home for the afternoon rest,
in the dim coolness, he shucks off
the heat's fiery caress and sleeps
wrapped in a dream fulfilled—
in charge
outdoors
away from an office
away from Los Angeles.

Late afternoon back to work
he watches the sun slide off
the bronze edge of the earth.
A star river pours
through the sky—enough light
to see the pump-jacks dip rise dip rise
like huge prehistoric horses.

First heard, then seen—
an explosion catapults
a derrick two hundred feet in the air.
Orange devours black, snuffs
the stars.

Fire roars for days burning
gas,
oil,
the job he loved
his life as he dreamed it.

Blue stars tumble from his eyes.

Exiled back to LA,
as the plane lowers, he ignores
the carpet of jewels spreading to infinity—
dark to him when he escaped,
dark to him still, a place
where the stars spill
out of the sky lighting up
sightless buildings selling
anything everything
except stars.

He turns away from the neon seduction.
He favors the gold shimmering
in a glass tumbler. When he drinks
enough, stars bloom
inside—all he needs
to get through the smog-clogged
days, the black soot of the night.
All he needs to keep from swallowing
pills the color of stars
without the shine.

*The Masjed Soleyman oil field is an Iranian oil field located in Masjed Soleyman, Khuzestan.

Without a Life Vest

My mother makes Christmas pies.
I eat leftover dough baked
with butter, cinnamon, sugar—
taste my mother's palm prints.

I hold the ribbon
while she ties bows on the presents.
Even though he never says it,
your dad loves you, she says.
Without moving her lips.

At summer's first touch,
I beg for bare feet to race
through sprinklers arcing rainbows.
I shuck shoes on the way
to the beach house. Three weeks—
my mother sweeps sand out the door,
reads novels, smokes cigarettes.
I wade in the lacy bones of spent waves,
collect unbroken scallop seashells,
wait for my father's weekend visits.

Sunday morning, he swings
me onto his shoulders, strides
into the heaving ocean.
I stretch my eyes wide open
as we climb water mountains
plunge down the trenches.
Over and over.

I turn eleven.
He loosens my grip finger by finger.
Without a life vest I fall.
I cannot stop falling. He doesn't see.

He looks at my mother
through a bottle of Jim Beam,
smiles a gold watered-down smile.
She fixes her eyes on his drinking mouth,
sometimes spies me from the corner
of her eyes bleeding tears.

Devil Doll

While my sister and I roll down
the forever front lawn,
in our bedroom Crazy Doll murders
our pretty dolls, maims the pretend babies,
bites holes in our biggest teddy bear.

We find her under the bed,
her tufted head turned away,
blue eyes glassed-over.
No use talking to her.
Our sentences rock and buckle.
Time to toss her into the closet asylum.

A few weeks later her sobs,
I've changed.
I will never again,
uncurl our rolled-up hearts.
We open the black-filled closet,
our forgiving hands free her.

Once again, we believe her.
Once again, we forgive her.

Again, Crazy Doll cracks.
Dead dolls litter the floor,
injured ones writhe when we daub
iodine on their open wounds.

Across my lap
Crazy Doll spread-eagles
The closet for the insane
does not a sane doll make,
I say to my little sister

who rounds her china-blue eyes,
leans close and whispers,
She is a devil-doll.

In the pantry under us,
heavy footfalls break the air.
A cupboard whines open,
the cork squeaks out of a bottle.

Through clenched teeth,
my sister squeezes the question,
Is Daddy drinking again?
For a second I forget how to breathe.

Crazy Doll squirms in my lap,
begs for another chance.
I shake her until her body whiplashes.
No…more…chances!
Off with your head!

My sister slits her eyes, licks her lips.
Yes, yes, she breathes.

A Wish Laid Bare

Erect as if her spine were steel,
my mother, in a black cocktail dress,
sips from a cut-glass champagne flute.
A starving man snatches her gaze,
loots her attention. His jowls jiggle
with greed as he gobbles her sympathy.

Her attention wobbles,
the smooth stretched across her face wavers.
Who can save her?
She searches for her husband—
handsome even though red lines
map his face. He functions
but only barely
as he fights the whiskey's grip.
He can't even save himself.

The ravenous man won't stop talking.
Words pile into her ears, tumble
onto the table. She stares
at the heaped utterances,
chokes on decadent-drenched air.
No one notices her small struggle
to catch her breath.

She declares to someone, to anyone,
I could have been an archeologist
in the red-gold desert searching
for artifacts; my fingers digging
in the copper sand for relics, bones,
and for my heart lost among ancient stones.

Guests stare at her wish laid bare.
Faster than the eye can follow, she paints
on a smile the color of a red tulip
and speaks in silvery tones,
Don't mind me.
It's the champagne talking.

The Hand-Off

The speedometer trembles at one-twenty
but the Cadillac runs smooth, silent
as my father steers left-handed,
his right arm draped
over the top of the front seat.

I want to touch that blond-furred arm,
hold his fingers in my hand's hollow.

My mother leans to the right,
stares out the front window at the black asphalt
unwinding into the desert's lusterless gold.
She doesn't look at him or at me
or at the fifth of whiskey
amber-stilled next to her left foot.

Out the window to the left,
a mountain presses purple up up
until lead clouds block the ascension
and, through that metallic gray,
God shoots silver shafts just for me.

Give me the bottle, Edith,
he says to my mother.
I see the dip of her left shoulder,
hear the slap of the bottle against his hand.

Her gaze never leaves the ochre-scrubbed sand.

He tilts the Jim Beam—
the scorched yellow liquid flows
into his mouth. I hear him gulp and swallow.
I see his fingers tender-curled
around the bottle's neck.

In the mirror his crow's feet gentle
and his dishwater eyes flash
a moment's burnished blue—
not for my mother not for me not for himself
not for the saffron sand or the purple mountain
but for the brown-gold whiskey.

Out the window—
still purple, the mountain—
the white-gold slashing the stubborn gray,
not god-painted or angel-mounted—
a trick of the atmosphere, a slight of the hand.

The Color of Goodbye

blue
the father's terrycloth robe
water-faded like his eyes

black and white
the police car where he sits with wrists
circled in handcuffs gun-metal grey

silver
the ropes of rain tangled
in the purple sky the daughter steers
through to bail out the father

white
the tablecloth and napkins
crumpled in the laundry room
not spread flat on the oak table
where the daughter and the mother drink
black coffee until the father calls
from the motel room
whispers *good bye I love you*

bone-white
the color of the pills scattered around
the half-filled bottle of whiskey tinted pyrite

colorless
the mother's whispered words
streaking down the grey-dimmed
hallway toward the yellow bathroom

green
the shade of the eye shadow the daughter applies
the color for *go-run-get-out-of-here*
from the mother's words before

he's dead he's dead
become the color she breathes forever.

After My Father's Suicide

My father's dead,
not gone. I know because
I see his upper body leaf-crowded;
his arms about to thin and divide into bent
and arcing branches; torso soon to thicken and
lengthen into a steadfast trunk. Leaves caress his face
and emboss their pattern on his shrinking skin. His watered-
down blue eyes round with fear and sorrow and regret
for kissing death on the mouth. Before stained
glass green usurps his sight, before leaves
curl through his nose, before stems
spiral down his throat, his words
flutter like the wind
ruffling
leaves.
Will I be
able to keep
my heart? No, the
tree answers, although you will spin rings throughout your being.

Like Father Like Daughter

Somewhere within me a river
heavy with black water surges,
heaves my dead father head first,
the whites of his eyes glinting.

It was not the drink that killed him,
although sufficient to shred his liver
black-out his heart,
gut his insides.

It was the white pills he swallowed—

all of them, a thousand of them.
Now he swims white in the dark river,
cries for me to get him out
or get in with him.

Death Takes My Mother

On the strands of a spider web
the sun plucks
an overture of light.
The sky's blue vibrates
and a nearby rose sings
a lipstick-red aria—

the color my mother wore,
although when dying,
her unpainted mouth radiated
pink that I kissed over and over
whispering *wake up wake up*
please wake up.

Center-stilled
in a light-storm of symmetry,
a spider waits for a passerby
who, blinded by the threads' flash,
will dive headfirst into the sink
of those sinuous strands.

My mother sways and stumbles
into the web's silken stick—
no fight, not even a token scuffle,
as the spider, jaws agape,
scuttle-stops,
scuttle-stops
nearer and nearer.
I shut my eyes, lay my face
against the rose of her cheeks—
so close to her soul
his fangs graze my heart.

Goodbye to Once Before

I buried my mother's remains next to my dad's and bled goodbye,
her grey-washed eyes, wobbly smile, heart-broken hands, I said
goodbye.

Her dust, gritty with bone flakes, breathed out of a brown
cardboard box,
ashes so fine they seeped out the telling cracks for a grave
goodbye.

When I last saw my mother still living, her once straight hair
white-whorled,
pink grazed her downy cheeks, she breathed out cinnamon and
sighed goodbye.

I kissed her rose-stained lips not cold, her face not bone-white with
absence,
no groan, no death rattle—just a faint buzz threading into goodbye.

Next to my father her boxed dust-body lies eternally stilled,
his body devoured by maggots and worms to feed the goodbye.

Once my father battered his being through the restraining order,
his right hook smashed the policeman's left jaw, an ill-fated
goodbye.

He wore his blue terrycloth robe for the ride to the city jail,
my mother and I drank black coffee and dark unsweetened
goodbyes.

The morning after the telephone rang out. He craved a Godspeed,
not for a day, a week, a month or a year—a forever dead goodbye.

My mother said, *No, don't! I love you, too,* and not one word more,
she hung up on a world of love forever and honeyed goodbyes.

My mother lived and died through that long obliterating goodbye,
I am still alive but sometimes pray for a splintered goodbye.

Oh, Momma, Tell Me Where You Are

While drying my hair
I ask the mirror,
Momma, do you remember
I cried when you tugged
my hair into pin curls?

I stopped when you said,
You will be beautiful.
Later you brushed out my hair
into a halo of pale curls.

Do you remember, Momma,
while eating lunch out,
we watched the sky shake loose
snowflakes larger than our salad plates?
Afterward we decorated the Christmas tree,
every ornament and every light placed
to shine the dark out of winter.

Now holiday trinkets crumple in boxes,
steel-plated clouds block the snowfall,
and the color of your drifting ashes dulls
the season's blues and silvers,
greens and reds.

Oh, Momma, tell me where you are.

Your answer rides a wind that breaks
the sky into pieces.

You will never find me.
I am where you are not,
a glint in a star's corona.

Please, Momma,
if you show me how to thread
through the twists and turns
of the Milky Way,
I will find you.

The White of My Mother's Hands

Snow splinters the winter light
into millions of micro suns.

No white is whiter.

Not the stars sequined sprinkle
nor wind-scudded clouds
nor the foam floating on the wave's edge.

Crows crackle their black
and shatter the white silence.

No black is blacker.

Not rain-slicked slate
nor the moon-absent night
nor coal glittering on hidden rock walls.

When we die, does the blackest of black
roll over us until we disappear
into a Vantablack abyss

or do we disintegrate into millions
of ions the sun scintillates
in the snow stretched over the lawn?

White seems a better way to go
until I think of my dead mother's hands—
the whitest of all.

Church of Trees

I believe in trees—
not God
not angels
although leafed-out branches
could be their wings.

The good don't go to heaven.
Their souls glide into oaks and aspens,
maples, elms, and birches
where they wind round and round
until they reach the heart of the tree.

My mother lives in a huge sheltering maple.
Into the wind she breathes messages
to swim into my body—
Next to me
grows an oak tree,
sturdy, well-rooted.
When you die,
float out of your body,
slide into that tree.
When, one day,
lightning
disease
or the axe
fells our trees,
our hearts
will surge through
the purple-bruised sky.
Near the center
of the Milky Way,
in a spiral's curve,
a binary star
will explode into being.

The Hereafter

I am nearing the dark.
Gathered in tight murders,
crows watch and bow
to the ink-stained cloud
closing in on me.

The sun casts a sidelong glance
then drops
to the other side of the world,
too bored with the dark,
too bored with me
to watch the gloom advancing.

As the coal-dark shadow approaches,
nearby stars watch,
pulse,
and scatter glitter,
coating my body in star-shed.

An angel spies my gleaming body—
not a sculpted angel
waving creamy wings.
An angel darker
than a black hole
folds me
into his stormy plumage,
flies me
to the star of his choice,
and flings me into a flare
erupting from the corona.

Beside me my mother flames.

The Skin of Her Eyelids

Sadness eclipses
the gray clarity
of her eyes
after he dies,
her husband,
my father.
Those eyes remember
him at the motel
    dead
by his own hand.

Pain burrs her voice
when she speaks
to me,
to my sister.
She thinks
she did not love
us enough,
him enough.

He is the one
who did not love enough.
He sloughed
his body
through a membrane
    thinner
than the skin
of her eyelids
and pushed his heart
where love
is blind,
love is deadlocked.

Before she left
her body,
her skin turned
gold and thin
like an autumn leaf
about to float
     down
or away
or somewhere,
maybe where
she is now

where
I want to be
if only the autumn sun
would burn
my skin gold.

Not Nothing

Sometimes something can be seen
through the bay window.
Is that rain? My husband asks.
No, a sort of scintilla,
tiny round speckles of not-nothing
crowding the air,
perhaps drifting souls of loved ones.

Have I not felt a whisper
brush my skin? A tingle
I cannot untangle?
If my mother, I would breathe her in.
She would fill me with grace.

About the Author

Pattie Palmer-Baker is a Portland, Oregon, artist, and poet. Over the years of exhibiting her artwork—a combination of paste paper collages with her poetry in calligraphic form—she discovered that many liked the poems better than visual art despite what people may believe. She now concentrates on writing both poetry and personal essays. Pattie has been nominated for the Pushcart Poetry Prize and published in many journals, including five *Poeming Pigeons Anthologies; Voicecatcher; The Best of Voicecatcher; Ghazal Page; Calyx; The Art and Science of Psychotherapy;* and *Phantom Drift.* She was the first prize winner in the 2016 *Timberline Review,* first and second prize and the Bivona prize for the best overall entry for the *Ageless Authors Anthology* 2019, and winner of the 2020 first prize in the Central Oregon Writers' Guild contest. She is also the *Del Sol* publication first prize winner for the most promising novel in 2018.

www.ingramcontent.com/pod-product-compliance
Lightning Source LLC
Chambersburg PA
CBHW031155090426
42738CB00008B/1341